MEANINGFUL

DYING

By: Dr. Ruth Benjamin (PhD)

(Clinical Psychologist)

MEANINGFUL DYING - An Introduction

Now wait a minute !

How can dying be meaningful?

Meaningful to who?

The person dying?

The relative?

Dying is the worst thing that can happen to anyone; the most meaningless experience that a person can have; the epitome of the removal of all meaning.

Don't tell me dying can be meaningful!

Isn't the title of this book a contradiction in terms?

Dying can't be meaningful.

Isn't dying the ultimate in meaninglessness?

Can we individually be an island of meaning in a sea of meaninglessness?

If we see dying as meaningless, perhaps we should see the whole world as meaningless, life as meaningless !

But dying CAN be meaningful; meaningful to the person, and, yes, meaningful to the relatives and friends. Sure, it is for those left behind a terrible, painful experience, but at the same time it can be filled with meaning, filled with memories that comfort and inspire long after the acute pain had dulled and the aching void is beginning to fade.

I want to take you with me to Grahamstown, South Africa, to Rhodes University. to a large lecture hall filled with students and staff. We are going back half a century, to some time in the 1960's.

A symposium is taking place, the title:

What is Death ?

What is Death ?

The large Lecture theatre was filled to capacity.

Everyone had a sense of expectancy.

The number of people interested had astounded the members of the Social Studies Group. It was a tiny struggling group where the new committee had planned the first meeting of the year and had hit on the title: "What is Death?"

They had arranged to have this in a smaller, group room which would comfortably accommodate between 15 and 20 people.

However, as students began to express interest in the upcoming symposium, in fact, even an excitement, the organizers had to move the future venue to a lecture theatre and to a larger lecture theatre and eventually to the largest lecture theatre. On the day of the symposium, that, too, was overflowing.

"What is Death?"

The speakers were very well selected.

The first was a Science Professor.

The second was a Prof. of Theology.

He third was a psychology lecturer, Dr. Marsh.

All were highly respected people in the world of academics.

The students were very enthusiastic about this subject which we had thought originally would hardly draw 30 people.

The hall was packed, in fact overflowing with students sitting on steps, square tables, and as a last resort, standing along the walls.

The Science Professor took the floor…

Now it has to be mentioned here: Science in those years had a somewhat dim view of anything spiritual or religious. It was before the years where scientists had discovered enough to realise that there were no glib answers as to how the world, an intricately perfectly formed running world had suddenly 'appeared.' (An organized, beautiful world was running like clockwork in an extremely complicated and effective way, which had to have at least some Intelligence or Super Intelligence behind it.)

In those days several decades ago, academics often viewed religion with a certain superiority, almost a pity for the person who needed to believe. Science held an indomitable place. Science was still the ultimate. There were some scientists who apologetically did believe, saying , usually, that they did this because they would not let religion enter their scientific world just as they would not let their scientific world corrupt or diminish their religious world.

This Science Professor at Rhodes University that day, was very clear in what he was saying:

What he said was interesting. He saw death as the ultimate end to the existence of a particular person. Once the heart stopped and respiration stopped there would be no more life, no more brain function. That would be impossible. The 'machine' had stopped for ever. But he also wanted to point out and make clear that we are all dying in fact we were decaying and dying from the day we were born.

Different cells would be dying off, replacing themselves regularly so that we did not die ultimately with the body we were born with. He then went further about scientific death leaving everyone with a strange sense of discomfort.

The Theology Professor was next, a medium slim man, pleasant enough. He spoke mostly about philosophy, using beautiful poetic English.

His discussion seemed to be very brilliant but very few people really understood what he was saying. And many just shook their heads in bewilderment.

And then came Dr. Marsh..... from the Psychology Department, except that his speciality was Parapsychology, the psychology of the 'unexplainable.' He was lecturing the 3rd year social work and psychology students and he was by far our favourite lecturer and his subject and its interpretation left us spellbound.

He came straight on the platform and told us a story , an incident that had happened to him several weeks before. I don't have his exact words. The whole symposium happened a long time ago. But I will write it as close to what he said as I can. I will try to put over some of the impact of what he was saying.
Incidentally another subject which he had studied and lectured on extensively was dreams and in this subject, too, he was dynamic.

"I want to tell you what happened to me last month," he started, after his introduction. " This kind of thing often happens to me , but this one was very interesting.

"Fairly early one morning a student came to me in a state of dread and anxiety. He had had a dream which was bothering him very much. He asked if he could please discuss the dream with me.

"I asked him to sit down, gave him some water and prepared to listen. The dream went something like this:

'Well,' said the young man. 'I know this might sound very strange. As you know I am a student in residence and my parents live fairly close by, in Port Elizabeth, and I often go home for the weekend, or if we have a few days off.

'Well I dreamed I was standing on a main road hitching, with all my necessary belongings in a knapsack on my back. It was a warmish day and I was just standing there hitch-hiking.

'Cars and cars came past and just no one seemed to be stopping for me. I might have been there for at least three quarters of an hour. But I stood there because usually I managed to eventually find a lift home.

'I waited...and waited... and then I saw a black Buick car . As it got nearer I saw it had a CB (Port Elizabeth) number plate. It stopped and the door opened and I saw two people in the car, a man and a woman.

'They were going all the way to Port Elizabeth and I was relieved to be going with them.

'However, as I began to get into the car it suddenly turned into a funeral car, a hearse.

'Then, Dr. Marsh, I woke up.'

His face had gone a deep red and he was breathing a little too fast. 'Dr. Marsh. It frightened me.'

'Why do you think it frightened you so much?'

'You see Dr. Marsh. I am going home today, right after I finish lectures and have some lunch. I will be hitch hiking back home. I will be hitching on that road.'
His voice trembled and he sounded very doubtful.

Dr. Marsh thought for a few moments.
'Go back to your residence and pack up as you usually would for hitch hiking and see what happens. After all you can always come back to Rhodes.'

Half an hour later the young man went to the road where he always hitched and stood on the pavement. The cars were going past and no one was stopping and he wondered if this time he was not going to get a ride.

He waited…..and waited………..and waited.

And then, there is was, a black Buick car with a CB number plate.

Trembling inwardly (and probably outwardly as well) he approached the car and saw the same man and woman he had seen in his dream, opening the door and preparing to welcome him into the car. This, to him, was terrifying!

Muttering some thanks but some excuse he ran back to Rhodes being very relieved that Dr. Marsh was still in his office.

He told him the story and Dr. Marsh told him to go back to his residence and he could prepare to hitch-hike later or even the next morning.

Some two hours later Dr. Marsh phoned the police.

Yes, a black Buick with a CB number plate had had a fatal accident further along that road. Both occupants of the car, a man and a woman had been instantly killed!

Dr. Marsh told two or three more true stories that day but I don't remember any of them. Only this story has remained with me in almost picture form.

There was a deathly hush after he had finished speaking as if something inside of them had been awakened and it had more of an impact because it had not come from a religious direction. It came from a totally scientific direction within the halls and context of a university.

The atmosphere in the lecture theatre had changed. This was different. He didn't tell us many stories that day, only a few, hand picked ones that he told us with a clarity that startled us. But they were powerful and his message was powerful.

As far as I know he was not a religious man, at least, not obviously so, but his message was strong and compelling.

Many years ago we assumed that science had all the answers and that we don't know them or they have not yet been discovered. Today someone who only knows a little bit of science might think that, but those who are the real scientific scholars know that is not true and there are more questions than answers . One can only describe rather than explain. The advent of Quantum Physics and Quantum Mechanics has only pointed further to the existence and involvement of a Higher Power.

Today's Scientific World is beginning to acknowledge a Higher Power. Scientists look at their textbooks and realise that they are not looking at the product of a random pot of ink falling over some random paper which would by chance be bound into a book,...Who would have that kind of faith?

Everything points in direction of a Creator, of a Higher Power. Even looking at the 'washing cycle' of a cat makes it obvious that there is, somewhere, a brilliant Programmer and Inventor.....far far more than that.
I have no difficulty in acknowledging that my washing machine came from Samsung and did not just evolve or come by chance, just as the cat's washing cycle did not come by chance.

Science is talking more and about miracles such as the miracle of migration.

Birds, annually fly thousands of miles along the same routes to warm climates, returning to their homes once winter has passed. Other animals do this also. No one has ever really found out how this works. However modern science in beginning to connect migration with quantum mechanics.

We have come a long way since that first symposium and there is a lot of research and examples pointing to a deeper reality.

Science has developed and has shifted away from being the major opponent of faith and the ever growing number of findings has confirmed a reality and a simple complexity and order in the world. Scientists like Prof. Herman Branover, (Physics) are able to work without any contradictions between Faith and Science.

Dr. Elizabeth Kubler Ross

Once upon a time, doctors did not tell people they were dying. It was not spoken about, and even direct questions by the dying person usually elicited negative answers.

Even when the person would say: "Doctor, I know I am dying", the doctor would negate this with a fatherly shake of his head (even if he were old enough to be the patient's grandchild) and chide her gently for thinking something so negative.

Today the thinking had generally changed (though it has not been entirely eradicated), and people are told their diagnosis and their prognosis (what to expect, medically, in the future).

True. families still try to hide it from the patient. We still often hear: "Don't tell him he has cancer. He couldn't take it".

They do not realize that it is THEY who do not know how to handle it or how to deal with a dying person. It is far too scary.

But more often now the person is told and some time after he (or she) is told he will start to go through various emotions and stages.

Dr. Elizabeth Kubler Ross, a Swiss psychiatrist, dedicated her life to work with Death and Dying. Her work in fact both pioneered and revitalized people's attitudes to the dying

She is famous for her five stages of dying and also of mourning, though she gave repeated warnings that a person did not HAVE to go through all the stages and they did not have to be in the order they were given.

Many of these "stages" overlap, occur together, or even some reactions are missed altogether.
They started off with shock and denial then rage and anger and then grief and pain.

Later they bargained with their Higher Power. They then got depressed 'why me?' and finally they withdrew into themselves for a time, separating from others while hopefully a stage of peace and acceptance would settle in.

(This is different to resignation. Resignation occurs when there is a lot of 'unfinished business')

Stages of Dying

Denial

Anger

Bargaining

Depression

Acceptance.

Denial.

But what is denial?

'I feel fine.'

'It can't be happening to me.'

'I have heard somewhere, somehow that I am dying. It can't be!'

This is a temporary defence for the individual, replaced with a heightened awareness of what is happening. Sometimes people just put it out of their mind often to their detriment because they avoid the hospital and their treatment and this for a time can even make them feel better till reality catches up with them. However even denial cannot last forever.

'No, not me.'

' Scans were not mine. Mixed up with someone else.'

Denial is a defence, a normal healthy way of coping with unexpected, horrible and sudden bad news.

It causes a person to oscillate between end to life and return to life as it as always been.

The first time you hear that you are dying, you definitely don't really hear it. Your relatives and friends and close ones don't really hear it. You tend to blank it all out.

Anger

This can be an extremely difficult phase.

When denial breaks down it is often replaced by anger.

Why me? Why not him?

There is often an anger at everyone who is healthy. The person can be horrible, and irrational.

Dr. Kubler Ross gives an important instruction:

THE PATIENT'S ANGER SHOULD NEVER BE TAKEN PERSONALLY.

This is difficult for doctors and staff and they have to learn to understand this.

Because of anger the person is very difficult to care for due to misplaced feelings of hate and envy. Any individual who symbolises life or energy can be subject to projected resentment and jealousy

Why me?

Not fair. Who is to blame?

This can be a very difficult phase for the patient and the relatives and friends.

Why me?

How can this happen to me?

Who is to blame?

The individual recognises that denial cannot continue.

Bargaining

I will give my life savings if this thing would just go.

This stage involves the hope that the individual can somehow postpone or delay death. Usually the bargain is made with a Higher Power. 'If I can delay death I will change.'

Often the person goes into alternative medicine, seeking another, 'natural' cure.

Let me live till my son gets married.

I will do anything if .... Let me live till...

Depression

I am going to lose everything.

There is absolutely devastating change.

There is no future.

Giving up on the past. What is the future?

Sorrow. I am deeply sad.

At some point the person is severely depressed by the huge change in life.

Giving up.

The illness is no longer denied.

Deterioration.

Financial burden.

Rejection (often without foundation.)

Acceptance.

Then finally, some kind of acceptance.

Its going to be OK.

I can't fight it so I may as well prepare for it.

The individual begins to come to terms with their mortality.

He or she is not depressed nor angry. It is the time of quiet just before the long journey.

Whatever will be will be.

Sometimes they come to the realization that though they are dying it would be possible for their lives to still have purpose.

They could be living until death. They still had a reason to keep living right until the final breath.

Around 1970 one of Dr. Kubler Ross' patients, a Mrs. Schwartz, was rushed to hospital in critical condition. She was put in a room, and before the doctors could arrive she felt herself floating out of her body. The arriving resuscitation team worked on her.

Somehow she watched from above in the room, heard and seemed to know what the team were thinking. She went back into her body but was pronounced dead. Only much later when they came to attend to the body did they see that she was actually alive.

When she reported what had happened, no one except Dr. Kubler Ross believed her.

This seems to have been one of the first recorded cases of a clinical death experience. No one wanted to accept it.

It was after this that Dr. Kubler Ross set out to study this apparently new phenomenon.

Since then many thousands of people have had clinical death experiences and have usually emerged with a need to change their lives for the better. They are far more willing to help or even dedicate their lives to the service of helping others.

Relatives, colleagues and friends have noticed the difference. They also no longer feared death.
"You are dead, you are dead, there is nothing" no longer rings true because most of these people have experienced some kind of miracle, some kind of awareness of closeness to a Higher Power (though they will not always admit it.)

And they are becoming aware that there is far more to life than this world and their five senses.

Let me give to you a striking example given by Dr. Kubler Ross, now the pioneer in the study of death and dying both in the objective and subjective sense.

She gives an example of a completely blind woman who died in a hospital bed surrounded by her relatives. She was revived with a defibrillator and when she woke up she described everything that happened in the greatest detail.

The woman reported that she left her body still lying in the hospital bed and rose to the corner of the room (this is reported constantly). Here she could see and observe everything that was happening to her.

This she could describe in detail. She could hear everything and SEE everything and on waking up she could describe everything everyone was wearing, the colours and the styles.

Inside her body she was completely blind. Outside of her body she could see everything.

When she awoke she was, of course, once again blind.

Another interesting and validated case of a clinical death experience was with a man who had been the victim of a 'hit and run' and was left dead on the road.

He was revived later by the paramedics and was able to tell them the registration number of the 'hit and run' car. The runaway driver was found and charged.

I am sure he accepted all this with a lot of shock and amazement.

The Clinical Death Experience

Dr. Robert Lanza, a foremost scientist declares that the answer to life after death lies in the science of Quantum Physics.

This book is not a religious one though of course all or most religions have some sort of an afterlife. Something deep inside the human psyche has a strong connection with it. I am coming in over here from the scientific point of view, giving solid, authenticated examples. In this book I am not coming from a religious direction.

In the Clinical Death Experience or the Near Death experience, people die clinically and come back with intricate details of people who met them, people who had lived decades ago before and only known to the older generation. When described they recognise them and confirm with the old photograph albums.

Very few people truly believe that death is actually the end.

As we realise how big the universe is we might get the impression that Our Higher Power is too great and distant and unreachable to have any real personal connection with us who are only a tiny dots of insignificance compared to all of this.

But then we look through a microscope and we find that even the smallest item has detail upon well structured and beautiful detail. Perhaps in doing this we can see how important each of us are in the larger picture.

One hears more and more today about the Clinical Death Experience. This has been called numerous things the most common of which are:

The clinical death Experience
The near death experience
The life after death experience (As Alon Anava puts it)

.

A clinical death experience refers to personal experiences associated with impending or actual death, encompassing multiple possible sensations including detachment from the body, feelings of levitation, total serenity, security, warmth, the experience of absolute dissolution, and the presence of a light.

These phenomena are usually reported after an individual has been pronounced clinically dead or very close to death.

From bright white lights to out-of-body sensations and feelings of life flashing before their eyes, experiences reported by people who have come close to death but survived are common the world over.

It is only recently that a small, humble looking machine called a defibrillator, could have such success in doing this. This machine literally calls a person back from the world of death to the world of life.

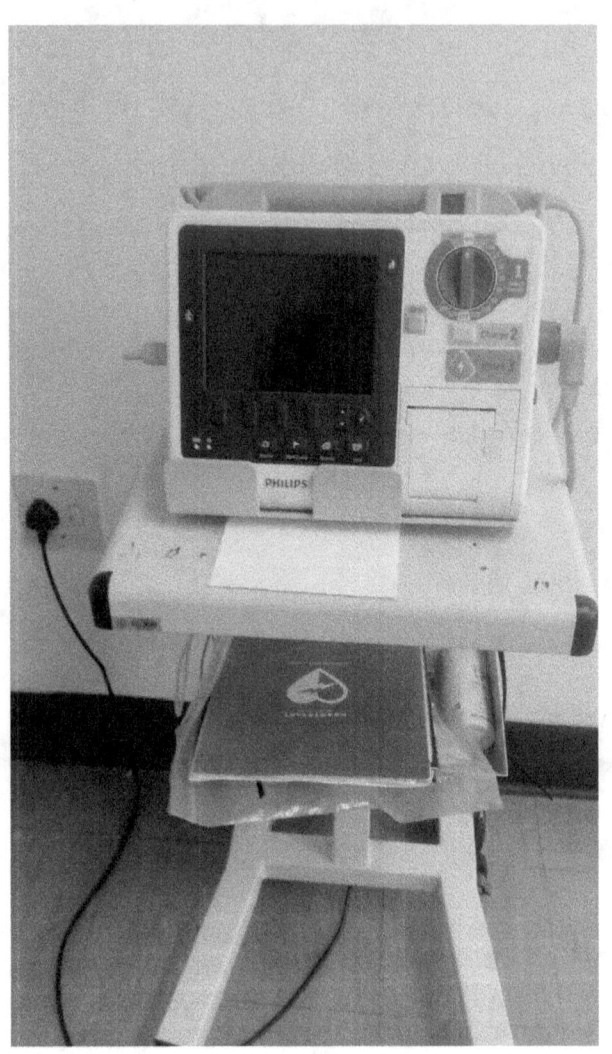

It restarts the heart and the respiration It changes a flat ECG to a normal ECG and very often the person wakes up at that moment often telling about very definite experiences they have had while they were dead, and they were dead according to all medical criteria. This is the defibrillator, now in many instances available not only in hospitals and clinics, but in community centres, places of worship, stations, universities, where people have been trained in the use of these things, usually a portable version of them.

The defibrillator literally brings people back from the dead. There are tens of thousands of people who are describing their clinical death experiences, though here I can describe only a few. Some of these involve situations where their objective reality and validity can be tested.

I believe that all of these stories hold validity and these are described by the people themselves in books, on websites and in magazines and scientific journals. Also people are more ready to talk about them so one might easily hear about these things, in conversation with a friend or chatting in the shops. These can also be researched and looked up.

I often wondered why it was that some people would return and wake up without any recollection at all about their clinical death. One day, while working in an office at the Hospital , I was looking with admiration at the defibrillator in the office. When a nursing sister came in I told her how amazing was this machine that it would bring a person from one world to another.

She told me that not many people wake up completely clear headed but would take time to do this. They would often be talking about religious things and about people (such as Abraham) who they had met. They would also often be talking about dead relatives and would talk in this confused way and only wake up properly some time later. I felt that was a very significant communication which must have a lot of significance and needs a lot of thinking about.

While many people are still skeptical of these accounts, others believe they offer the most definitive proof of life after death we might ever encounter.

And though the debate continues, one thing is for certain: These people insist what they went through was life-altering, and very very real.

On the 'Humans" website, Shawn Larson mentions Colton , who wasn't quite four years old when his appendix burst, landing him in a hospital for emergency surgery. On awakening he described a near death experience where he saw family members who had passed away previously—including a baby sister that his mother had lost due to a miscarriage. Neither of his parents had ever mentioned the miscarriage to him. He also met a man he called "Pop," whom he had seen in the other world as a young man. Later, he was able to identify Pop in a family photograph as the man he had seen in heaven. It was his paternal grandfather. And while the surgery was taking place, Colton told his father that he had seen him in another room, where he had gone to pray.

At this point his parents knew he was not making this up because he was able to tell them what they were doing in another part of the hospital.

In many of these experiences the person testifying finds it impossible to find human words to describe things (e.g. Alon Anava).

One woman found that in this state she had 500 senses instead of this world's five.

Anita Moorjani, an ethnic Indian woman from Hong Kong, author of "Dying to be Me" published by Hay Press, had end stage cancer (Hodgkin's Lymphoma) and was being cared for at home, but on the morning of February 2, 2006 she did not wake up.

She had fallen into a coma. Doctors said she would not make it beyond the next 36 hours since her organs were no longer functioning and her body had started to swell up, creating open skin lesions.

In spite of this, Anita saw and heard the conversations between her husband and the doctors that were taking place outside her room about 40 feet away down a hallway.

She also saw her brother on a plane, having heard the news that she was dying, coming to see her. Both things were later confirmed.

Four years old Adam had an accident and recalled his near death experience. "Right there I began floating above my body just watching, without being worried, just watching as they put me on the stretcher. They put me in the ambulance truck and I couldn't see inside, then I remember just being in a light for a while. "

In these examples there was some objective confirmation that the people were truly reporting what they saw and that they did have some access to what was happening even though there was no actual brain function.

There is both objective and subjective reality.

Subjective reality is with ME. I experience something, something very real to me but then is no way to validate objectively what I am seeing. Objective reality means that there are things that I can validate and check up on, as was done in several of the cases.

Alon Anava, in one of the clearest and in depth accounts of his after death experience as he called it (before he returned to this life), says how he himself validated some of the things he had experienced, for instance with the person in the taxi with him. He could, during his death experience, see her whole life spread before him and afterwards he validated it with her and it was completely correct in every detail and he had not known any of this before. Also he had learned a lot on the other side which he had never known before and this was validated by his subsequent teachers.

He had difficulty finding even inadequate words to describe his experiences. English was inadequate.

The 'clinical death experience' reported by cardiac arrest survivors worldwide is now being grounded in science, according to research conducted at the University of Michigan Health System. They feel they have come further in clarifying why the brain continues to function well after clinical death.

There has been a lot of controversy as to whether and how the dying brain is capable of generating conscious activity. This study was done on animals.

The University of Michigan study shows that shortly after clinical death, in which the heart stops beating and blood stops flowing to the brain, rats display brain activity patterns characteristic of conscious perception.

For some scientists, seeing the light during near death experiences is only associated with the brain's attempt to create electrical activity. For many others, there's much more to it.

These scientists are coming to believe that near-death experiences cannot be considered as something imagined. On the contrary, the origins could lead them to be perceived although not lived in this reality, but another.

In this study researchers analysed the recordings of brain activity called electroencephalograms (EEGs) from nine anesthetized rats undergoing experimentally induced cardiac arrest.

Within the first 30 seconds after cardiac arrest, all of the rats displayed a widespread, transient surge of highly synchronized brain activity that had features associated with a highly aroused brain.

The brain is assumed to be inactive during cardiac arrest. However this was the first in depth study of the neurophysiological state of the brain immediately following cardiac arrest which prior to this had not been systemically investigated .

They were surprised at the actual levels of brain activity , levels that exceeded even the normal waking state. In other words the 'DEAD' brain at this stage was more active than the LIVING AWAKE brain.

This doesn't mean clinical death experiences are imagined or that the brain creates an experience that is imagined, but it tells us that there is clinical evidence of something occurring within the brain that should be otherwise impossible according to what we have previously known about the brain.

Dr. Michael Sabom , a cardiologist gives a detailed medical and scientific analysis of an amazing clinical death experience of a woman named Pam .

She underwent a rare operation to remove a giant **basilar artery aneurysm** in her brain that threatened her life. It was not safe to use standard neuro-surgical techniques to remove it.

She was referred for an operation known **hypothermic cardiac arrest**. This operation, nicknamed "standstill" by the doctors who perform it, required that Pam's body temperature be lowered to 60 degrees, her heartbeat and breathing stopped, her brain waves flattened, and the blood drained from her head.

In our terms this means, she was put to death. After removing the aneurysm, she was restored to life. During the time that Pam was in standstill, she had a clinical death experience. Her out-of-body observations during her surgery were later verified to be very accurate. This case is considered to be one of the strongest cases of veridical evidence in clinical death experience research because of her ability to describe the unique surgical instruments and procedures used and her ability to describe in detail these events while she was clinically and brain dead.

Pam heard and reported later what the nurses in the operating room had said and exactly what was happening during the operation. At this time, every monitor attached to Pam's body registered "no life" whatsoever. At some point, Pam's consciousness floated out of the operating room and travelled down a tunnel which had a light at the end of it where her deceased relatives and friends were waiting including her long-dead grandmother. Pam's clinical death experience ended when her deceased uncle led her back to her body for her to re-enter it. She was able to remember and report all this accurately.

A similar operation was described by Prof. Shimon Silman where he gave more details about the patient's condition at the time. The heart is stopped, the brain waves cease and at that point the patient is scientifically and legally dead. When a reporter asked the patient how she felt about the fact that she was 'dead' during the procedure she responded simply "I am alive now." This operation took place at Columbia University Hospital .

Perhaps the largest scientific and medical study into near-death and out-of-body experiences was conducted by scientists at the University of Southampton. They spent four years examining more than 2,000 people who suffered cardiac arrests at 15 hospitals in the UK, US and Austria. They found that nearly 40 per cent of people who survived described some kind of 'awareness' during the time when they were clinically dead before their hearts were restarted. They also discovered clinically that some awareness may continue even after the brain has shut down completely.

One man in the study even recalled leaving his body entirely and watching his resuscitation from the corner of the room.

Despite being unconscious and 'dead' for three minutes, the 57-year-old social worker from Southampton, recounted the actions of the nursing staff in detail and described the sound of the machines.

"We know the brain can't function when the heart has stopped beating," said Dr Sam Parnia, a former research fellow at Southampton University, now at the State University of New York, who led the study.

"But in this case, conscious awareness appears to have continued for up to three minutes into the period when the heart wasn't beating, even though the brain typically shuts down within 20-30 seconds after the heart has stopped.

"The man described everything that had happened in the room, but importantly, he heard two bleeps from a machine that makes a noise at three minute intervals. So we could time how long the experience lasted for.

"He seemed very credible and everything that he said had happened to him had actually happened." They found that out later.

Dying.

Dr. Randy Pausch was at the height of his career at Carnegie Mellon University when he was diagnosed with pancreatic cancer and given a year or so to live. After the initial shock he decided to give all he could to his remaining life, all he could for his wife and family, all he could for his students and all he could for the world at large. Dynamic as he was before , the impetus of his 'dying status' made him more dynamic. He gave a lecture at his University called "The Last Lecture.

Really Achieving Your Childhood Dreams." In this lecture he was inspirational, dynamic and compelling. The force of his personality and his strength of character shone through as he showed how determined he was to follow and fulfil his dreams and he showed how a brick wall was only a challenge to a person who would not give up. He was honest in his assessment of his life and had a sense of humour which drew him closer to his audience.

He also published a book entitled "The Last Lecture" which became a best seller. At one of his later Last Lectures he did push-ups on the stage and offered inspirational life lessons. As he said, he became by this an 'accidental celebrity.'

Close to his death there was another Last Lecture.

He mentioned the things he could do to make a difference to his wife, his children and his students.

For his children especially he wanted them to know he never gave up and he wanted them to know how much he loved them and that wherever he would be he would be looking and watching and being incredibly proud of them even though at that moment he was very sad he was not right by them.

He told his wife how much he loved her and how much he wanted her to be happy.

He left for his students and other students, a program called 'Alice' which would teach animation and anyone and everyone could download it from the University and they would continue to develop and support it.

People from his university also pledged to do things in his name.

There was a university lecturer who had terminal cancer. Her two children were aged 13 and 10 and she knew that over time their memory of her would become duller. She therefore made a book, a kind of scrapbook, individually for both of them with photographs of all different things and a lot of the family together and of places they visited.

She gave them an insight into who she was and how she had studied and what was important to her and how she loved her children.

She mentioned various talents which they could look for and maybe discover within themselves. She told them about her family and how she grew up. She told them how she had met their father and had truly loved him. She told them important and heart warming details of all their lives which they needed to keep in their memories.

Once a person is told and has more or less accepted that they are dying it is important to prepare for the journey in a meaningful way and eventually to talk to others about it.

Financial things are important to take care of, especially if the person is the head of a household. One makes a will on a financial and 'possessions' level but there is another type of will, in many respects just as important.

How do you want to be remembered? What you say here will stick with and influence everyone.

A message to people who are precious to you is something that will guide and inspire them.

At this time your words are weighted in gold.

Make that second type of will.

Make a will of good thoughts and positive encouragement for the people left behind

For the younger children or your descendants....especially close younger children; so many important things could be left for them to see and absorb later.

Most religions have, to some extent, before death, a concept of cleansing of oneself, of making an account of what a person would like to do or like to change before he or she enters the world of truth. We also need to deal with resentment and bitterness which has been with us our whole lives. This is different to the anger stage. It might be that there are people we no longer speak to and sometimes it is important to reconnect and to heal the wounds of the past.

Lets face it. We would all do better if we did that. But one would have to do this in a calm and settled frame of mind. As I mention, only do these things when you have the strength to do so and only do it one at a time. You are basically doing it for them but in a deeper stronger way you are doing it for yourself because there is a great satisfaction in '**unhurting**' someone. Each letter written or phone call made to perceived enemies can bring a deep sense of peace

We can assist with this even in the angry phase.

Don't leave hurt or bitterness whatever you do. What for?

At this point I want to look at the question of anger but not in the context of the Angry Stage, which will eventually pass.

This is a far deeper level of anger and it is important at any stage of life to deal with it.

A woman once came to me for therapy. Strangely enough (as you will see) she was brought on many occasions by her father.

Sometime during one of the sessions she mentioned that her father appeared to be quite friendly and caring, but for 15 years he had been in her home for only a few minutes at a time and consistently refused all invitations to eat with herself, her husband and her family. She said that this upset her very much.

I asked her why this was so and she replied that she had no idea at all about the reason.

I asked her permission to speak to her father and called him in by himself, asking him why he did not eat in his daughter's home.

Immediately he became emotional, telling me that 15 years ago his daughter had said something to him which had hurt him and he decided that until he received an apology he would not eat in her house. I asked him if his daughter was aware of this and he shook his head, telling me again that until she apologized he would not eat in her house. He could not actually remember what it was she had said.

I then requested his permission to speak with her.

I did, alone. She was flabbergasted, saying she hadn't known about this at all, and of course she would apologize!

I brought him in, she apologized and he immediately burst into tears, saying that he had waited for this for 15 years. But he hadn't told her! He had remained with his bitterness and resentment and hurt all those years, and deprived himself and his family of so much.

In one of my groups with my students I told this story and asked if anyone in the class was resenting someone and hadn't spoken about it. One of the girls volunteered immediately that she had been a good friend of another girl in the class, but they had not been friends for a year. She mentioned the name of the girl, who turned to her in astonishment.

"I know you have become less friendly and you don't want to talk to me, but I don't know why?"

"You kicked me!" said the student.

The second student frowned, trying to search her memory. "I didn't," she said at last, "when did I kick you?"

The student mentioned the occasion and her ex-friend looked at her in horror. "I didn't kick you, I tripped over you. I said sorry, didn't I?"

Needless to say they sorted this out and they once again became friends, but it could so easily still have been otherwise.

There are various things one could do about these long lasting hurts and bitterness.

Try to unhurt, to sort out.
Don't be afraid to sort out resentment and bad relationships..

I am writing here about the person who becomes angry or upset at another person, doesn't explain to the person what has offended or angered him and withdraws, filled with deepening hurt, resentment and hatred. In his mind the upset builds up into something greater and more monstrous as he tries to justify his feeling.

The friend or relative in turn might ask what is wrong, but the person refuses to tell him, feeling that just as it pervades his mind, so it should pervade the friend's mind, so how could he not know, and the friend, too eventually withdraws. A rift is caused which becomes wider and wider. Bitterness holds the first person in its corrosive grip.

If we were to sift through our past we would probably find several people that we had distanced from because they had hurt us and we had become angry, upset or bitter. Some of us are more prone to it than others, but it affects everyone.

Perhaps we don't go to the extreme of cutting off our own close relatives to whom we no longer speak. Maybe former friends, people who were good friends, whom we no longer have contact with because of this; perhaps we are both losing out on a friendship which could be rewarding and fulfilling.

If we are resentful or hating someone or bitter or have

assumed that a person meant `this and this' when in fact they meant `that and that' and we have taken offence, we might hate to face the fact that though it might in some way affect that person, the real damage is done to ourselves.

As I said, bitterness is corrosive and it affects us probably on a spiritual, as well as on an emotional and even on a physical level.

Many people tend to `bottle up' anger until it becomes a seething mass of hatred and bitterness.

They accept insults and outwardly smile, but their inside `store' boils and bubbles.

I saw, and immediately copied an anonymous quotation on someone's notice board:

"Anger and bitterness do more harm to the vessel in which it is stored than the vessel over which it is poured."

Anger does not always have to be LET OUT. It can also be LET GO.

We need to sift through the past with a sieve which `catches' resentment and bitterness, analyzing and examining as many situations as possible which provoked this.

At times a person can see that his anger was not necessary and his more mature mind can see what the child or young person did not see, and in this way, he or she can let go.

Sometimes the person finds he can finally forgive an offending party. At times the person finds that though he still has to work on forgiving, he can agree to let go of his anger and to be willing to go on an extensive `cleaning up of the past'.

We can go on a 'search' for lost family and friends. The 'last bitter words' are explored, analyzed and perhaps understood in a completely different light. The person makes moves towards the person or persons, and very often friendships are reinstated and families are united, often with a deeper appreciation and understanding of one another.

To sort this out makes all the difference in the world. It is well worth the effort. You only really find this out when you start doing it. It is important to concentrate on the positive.

WHERE TO NOW?

Dr. Atul Gawande, a Harvard doctor gave a call to rethink dying as a meaningful part of life.

He started to really talk to the patients and started researching the end of life like a reporter would do and this took him into houses, nursing homes, and assisted living facilities, places where most doctors don't go

He came to a very important conclusion which points to a very real problem which arises between the older or dying patient and their loving, caring and responsible children. "Their children want them to be safe," Gawande said, but what older people want for themselves -- what we all want for ourselves -- is autonomy and a sense of purpose."

Here he opened up a brilliant insight ! No matter how old, no matter how sick (and usually the person most times does not feel old or sick), the person needs to do something meaningful, to study something interesting and worth while, to do some of the things they have always wanted to do.

Yes they do need to feel safe in that they have their living requirements, but at the same time they need freedom and independence.

He felt that better care would flow from awareness, talking about what makes life meaningful and what reduces suffering when time is short. The "fundamental barrier" to change, he said, is not money, but rather in the attitude of the people around.

FIFTY YEARS LATER

At the beginning of this book we went to a symposium at Rhodes University and heard a science professor who stated conclusively that death was the end of life.

This took place about 50 years ago at least.

Times have changed. Research methods have changed and scientific thought has developed and changed.

In the words of Dr. Arnie Gotfried, an ecologist and a brilliant scientist, "the most brilliant minds of 50 years ago could not even dream of the wonders of science and technology today."

He said that Science had come to a new found humility based on a recognition that all of its laws are in essence beyond rational comprehension altogether.

Biologists had described the origin of life as some random occurrence in a dead universe, but had no real understanding of how life began or how the universe appears to have been exquisitely designed for its emergence.

However the new world view is completely based on science and is better supported by the scientific evidence than traditional explanations. It challenges us to fully accept the implications of the latest scientific findings in fields ranging from plant biology and cosmology to quantum entanglement and consciousness.

If you listen to what the science is telling us now, it becomes ever more clear that life and consciousness are fundamental to any true understanding of the universe.

Prof. Robert Lanza, one of the most respected scientists in the world today states that new scientific theory says that we are immortal and exist outside of time.

I think that most people have had some kind of experience or awareness where they came to KNOW that there is a Higher Power who is available to them and concerned with them. They know they can have a personal connection with that Higher Power.

Perhaps this has faded somewhat in their minds but some thinking about it can reactivate it. They would not have admitted it to anyone. Often they admit it to me as a psychologist.

I am not asking you to admit it to anyone. If it bothers you no one else will know that you are beginning to talk to and communicate with and get close to your Higher Power. But you will know, and you will feel it.

I have spoken to many people about their clinical death experiences. (I can see, by the way, that they tend to tell very few people about these experiences. It is something very close and very real to them and to see disbelief or even pity on the face of someone close to them as they hear about these experiences is more than they can bear.)

But one and all describe it as giving them an inspiration and a faith which they had not had before and all describe it as a life changing experience, which is often born out by the observations of those abound them. They even seem to have within them a new dimension of compassion and caring and sensitivity where they themselves notice the difference. There is often a difference in the way they react to others, in fact the way they react to their surroundings. All say that they no longer in any way fear death.

They all see it as defining and significant in their lives. Time becomes elastic during these experiences. The person describes the sense of things taking hours whereas the actual clinical death could have been minutes.

There is a defibrillator in the office I use when I see patients at the Hospital. As I say again, I have a great respect for it.

As mentioned, Prof Robert Lanza is considered one of the leading scientists in the world. He is Chief Scientific Officer at the Astellas Institute for Regenerative Medicine and Prof. at Wake Forest School of Medicine.

"BIOCENTRISM", shocked the world with a radical rethinking of the nature of reality ... but that was just the beginning.

His latest book, BEYOND BIOCENTRISM, 2016, starts by acknowledging that our existing model of reality is looking increasingly creaky in the face of recent scientific discoveries. Biologists describe the origin of life as a random occurrence in a dead universe, but we have no real understanding of how life began, or why the universe appears to be exquisitely designed for the emergence of life.

'Biocentrism isn't a rejection of science. Rather, biocentrism challenges us to fully accept the implications of the latest scientific findings in fields ranging from plant biology and cosmology to quantum entanglement and consciousness.'

'By listening to what the science is telling us, it becomes increasingly clear that life and consciousness are fundamental to any true understanding of the universe. This forces a fundamental rethinking of everything we thought we knew about life, death, and our place in the universe.'

New scientific theory says we're immortal and exist outside of time

In an article describing his work it is shown that the problem is that the standard scientific paradigm doesn't recognize the spiritual dimension of life. "We're told we're just the activity of carbon and some proteins; we live awhile and die. And the universe? It too has no meaning. It has all been worked out in the equations – no need for a soul."

But biocentrism – a new 'theory of everything' – challenges this traditional, materialistic model of reality. In all directions, this outdated paradigm leads to insoluble enigmas, to ideas that are ultimately irrational. But knowledge is the prelude to wisdom, and soon our worldview will catch up with the facts.

He showed that our current worldview – the world of objectivity and naïve realism – is beginning to show fatal cracks

Though some may hold on to their older way of thinking, many cutting edge scientists are writing this way.

Anyone interested in following this up could Google 'Dr. Robert Lanza'   to be taken into the exciting world of Quantum Mechanics and Quantum Physics.

Many of us will find we can understand it.

When she first wrote her book on Dying and introduced the stages Dr. Elizabeth Kubler Ross wrote that she did not believe in an afterlife at all. Over the years and over her contact with thousands of dying patients, she began to believe in it absolutely. In her book The Wheel of Life of 1997 she declares that death is but a transition from this life to another existence; that Death is just a transition from this life to another existence where there is no more pain and anguish.

One of her last statements in the book reads as follows:

'Death is nothing to fear. It can be the most wonderful experience of your life. It all depends on how you have lived'.